Conte

The haircut *John Escott*	2
London *Christine Butterworth*	8
Wales *Christine Butterworth*	15
Mrs Peck-Pigeon *Eleanor Farjeon*	22
Ball bounce rhyme *John Cunliffe*	24
Northern Ireland *Jane Francis*	26
The Giant's Causeway *Traditional*	30
Edinburgh *Christine Butterworth*	34

The haircut

"You need a haircut, Mark," said Mum. "It's time you went to the barber."

"I don't like going to the barber!" said Mark. "He lets the hair get down my neck."

Mum thought about this. "You could go to the lady who cut my hair," she said.

"She will get hair down my neck, too!" said Mark.

"All right," said Mum. "Then I'll cut it."

Mark looked at her. "Can you cut hair?"

Mum smiled. "We'll soon find out," she said.

Mum put a sheet on the floor.

"Sit down," she said. Then she put another sheet over Mark to catch the hair.

"I hope you won't get hair down my neck," said Mark.

"I'll try not to," said Mum. "Now keep your head still." She got some scissors and began cutting Mark's hair. SNIP-SNIP-SNIP!

"I hope you know what you're doing," said Mark.

"Just don't move," said Mum.

Up-and-down-and-over Mark's hair went the scissors. SNIP-SNIP-SNIP! Mum was good at cutting the hedge. She was good at cutting the grass. But she was not very good at cutting hair.

"Oh dear," she thought. "What will Mark's hair look like when I've finished? I hope it's all right."

When she had finished, Mark looked in the mirror.

"My hair!" he shouted. "It doesn't look right! It's all ... funny! Everyone will laugh at me!"

He wanted to run away and hide. He wanted to put a paper bag over his head. He wanted to go and live on the moon. He didn't want to go to school – ever again!

"Take me to the barber!" he shouted.

"It's too late now, Mark," said Mum. "But I'll take you after school."

Mark got a surprise at school. His friends didn't laugh at him.

"I like your new haircut!" said Joe.

"Do ... do you?" said Mark.

"Which barber did you go to?" asked Paul.

"I didn't," said Mark. "My Mum cut it."

"It's great" said Jenny. "I've never seen one like it anywhere."

Mum came to meet Mark from school.

"I'll take you to the barber now," she said.

"No, it's all right," said Mark. "But ..."

"What is it, Mark?" said Mum.

"Can you cut Joe's hair the same way?" said Mark. "And Paul's, and Jenny's?"

"Oh dear," said Mum.

London

Big Ben and the Houses of Parliament.

London is one of the biggest cities in the world. Lots of people live and work in London, and many more go there on holiday.

People go to see old buildings such as the Houses of Parliament. These are by the River Thames. Near to them is a tall clock tower called Big Ben.

Tower Bridge opens to let big boats through.

Not far down the river are the Tower of London and Tower Bridge. There is a road across Tower Bridge. When a big boat comes up the river, all the cars have to stop and the bridge lifts up to let the boats go through.

The Tower of London was a prison long ago. Very special prisoners, such as kings and queens, were kept there.

Many people go to work in London each day. Lots of them go by Underground train. These trains run in tunnels far under the streets. To get to the trains, people have to go down in lifts or take the moving steps. These moving steps are called escalators.

There are other tunnels that take roads under the River Thames. The Underground trains and the roads get very busy when people are in a rush to get to work or to go home. This time of day is called the rush hour.

Diplodocus and Triceratops skeletons.

Many people go to London on holiday. There are lots of things to do if you are on holiday. London has many big museums where you can see old things. In one of the museums you can find out about dinosaurs and other animals.

St. Paul's Cathedral

There are lots of big buildings in London. One of the big churches is called Saint Paul's. You can go up lots of steps to get to the top of Saint Paul's. Then you can look out over London.

The Peter Pan statue is in Kensington Gardens.

People are never far from a big park in London. It's fun to take a picnic to the park and feed the ducks. In some parks people can take boats out, or ride horses. If it is hot they can even go for a swim. Some people like to take a boat trip on the River Thames.

There are interesting statues to see in some of the parks. There is a statue of Peter Pan in a park called Kensington Gardens.

    People who are on holiday like to go shopping to get presents for their friends. The biggest toy shop in the world is in London.

    The streets of London are still busy at night. People like to go to a restaurant or go to see a play.

    There is always something to do in London.

Wales

Pier Head House, Cardiff Docks.

Wales is the smallest country in Britain. The capital city of Wales is Cardiff. Cardiff is by the sea and the city has big docks. Boats from all over the world come in and go out of Cardiff docks.

Raglan Castle, Gwent

Cardiff Castle, South Glamorgan

Kidwelly Castle, Dyfed

Beaumaris Castle, Anglesey

Cardiff has many new buildings and an old castle. There are lots of castles in Wales. Some were built long ago by Welsh princes. Some were built by the kings of England.

Caernarfon Castle

One of the biggest castles in Wales is in Caernarfon. It was built by an English king called King Edward. He wanted to be King of Wales, too, so he built a strong castle for his English soldiers. He built a town by the castle, with walls all round it.

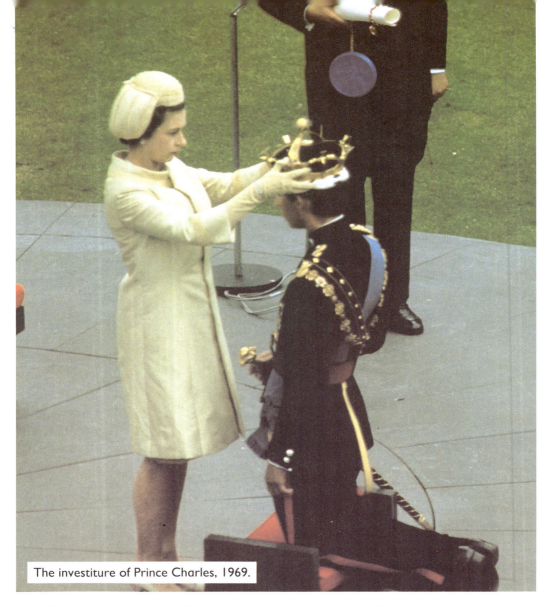

The investiture of Prince Charles, 1969.

King Edward called his baby son the Prince of Wales. Ever since then, all the English kings and queens have called their oldest son the Prince of Wales.

In 1969 the Queen came to Caernarfon Castle and made Prince Charles the Prince of Wales.

Mount Snowdon is the highest mountain in Wales.

Many people go on holiday to Wales. Some of them go to climb the mountains. The highest mountain in Wales is near Caernarfon. It is called Mount Snowdon. People who don't want to climb up Mount Snowdon can get to the top in a little train.

The slate caverns museum, Blaenau.

Near Mount Snowdon there is a village called Blaenau. There are big caves under the mountain at Blaenau. The walls of the caves are made of slate. Men used to dig out the slate. Then they took it by train to the sea and put it on to the ships. The ships took the slate all over the world. Slate was used to make roofs.

Now visitors can go to see the slate caves.

People in some parts of Wales speak Welsh. All the children in Wales learn Welsh at school. Welsh people have their own television and radio in Welsh. The road signs are in English and Welsh.

Every year there is a big festival in Wales. Singers come from all over the world. There is a prize for the best poem in Welsh. The winner gets a silver crown.

Mrs Peck-Pigeon

Mrs Peck-Pigeon
Is picking for bread,
Bob-bob-bob
Goes her little round head.
Tame as a pussy-cat
In the street,
Step-step-step
Go her little red feet.
With her little red feet
And her little round head,
Mrs Peck-Pigeon
Goes picking for bread.

Eleanor Farjeon

Ball bounce rhyme

Let's catch a bus
And go to town,
And ride the escalators
Up and down.

Up and down
And home again,
Jumping puddles
In the rain.

Home to chips
And a cup of tea,
Watching films
On the old tv.

John Cunliffe

Northern Ireland

There are giant cranes at Belfast Docks.

Belfast is the capital city of Northern Ireland. It is by the sea and it has big docks where ships are made. Belfast is famous for building ships.

There are some giant cranes at the docks. They are used to lift heavy things on and off the ships.

The City Hall, Belfast.

Belfast is the biggest city in Northern Ireland. It has many tall buildings and busy shops. The City Hall is one of the most beautiful buildings in Belfast.

There aren't many big cities in Northern Ireland, but there are lots of beautiful places to see in the countryside.

The Giant's Causeway, County Antrim.

This picture shows a place by the sea called the Giant's Causeway. It looks like a big path made out of rocks. The path goes along the cliffs and out into the sea.

There is an old story which says that the Giant's Causeway was a path made by a giant called Finn MacCool. The story says that the path went all the way across the sea from Ireland to Scotland.

The Causeway is made from volcanic rock.

People still tell the story of Finn MacCool, but now people think that the Giant's Causeway was made by a volcano. Thousands of years ago a volcano exploded and the hot rock ran over the land like a river. When the rock cooled down, it went hard and cracked.

The Giant's Causeway

There was once a giant called Finn MacCool. He was the biggest and strongest giant in Ireland.

Finn heard that there was a giant in Scotland who wanted to fight him. Finn was not frightened. He wanted to meet the Scottish giant so he started to build a path from Ireland to Scotland. He used big rocks to build a causeway across the sea. When the Scottish giant heard about Finn's causeway, he started to build a causeway from Scotland to Ireland.

One day, Finn's wife came to tell him some news. She had heard that the Scottish giant was even bigger and even stronger than Finn! They looked out across the sea. Far away, they could see the giant coming across the causeway.

Finn ran back along the causeway to his home. He was a very clever giant and soon he thought of a trick to play on the Scottish giant. Quickly, he found some giant baby clothes and put them on. Then he jumped into a cot and waited for the Scottish giant.

Soon the Scottish giant came to the door.

"I have come to see Finn MacCool!" he said, in his giant voice. "Where is he?"

"He's not at home," said Finn's wife. "He has gone out for a walk. Would you like to wait for him?"

Just then, Finn started to make a noise like a baby crying.

"Who is that crying?" asked the Scottish giant.

"That's just our baby," said Finn's wife. The Scottish giant looked at the great big baby in the cot.

"If that is the baby, how big must the father be?" he thought.

The Scottish giant started to feel frightened. He turned round and ran back across the causeway to his home in Scotland. On his way, he pulled up the rocks of the path and threw them into the sea so that Finn couldn't come after him.

And that is why only the two ends of the causeway are left. You can see one end in Northern Ireland and the other on the Isle of Staffa in Scotland.

Edinburgh

Edinburgh Castle and the Scottish National Gallery.

Edinburgh is the capital city of Scotland. Long ago, people in Scotland had their own kings and queens. The parliament of Scotland was in Edinburgh. Many people go to Edinburgh to see the old buildings.

There is a big castle in the old part of Edinburgh. Soldiers still live in the castle, and the crown jewels of Scotland are kept there. There are many old guns around the castle.

Holyrood Palace

Edinburgh Castle is on a hill. A long street goes down the hill to Holyrood Palace. When the Queen goes to Edinburgh she stays in Holyrood Palace. The long street is called the Royal Mile.

By the Royal Mile are small streets with tall old houses. Each little street is called a close. Long ago lots of people lived in each house and every close was very crowded.

The statue of Greyfriars Bobby.

Many visitors go to Edinburgh to see Greyfriars Church. By the church is the statue of a dog called Greyfriars Bobby. Bobby lived long ago. He was a policeman's watch-dog. When the policeman died, Bobby came to keep watch over his grave. Bobby kept watch for many years until he died too. People put up a statue of Greyfriars Bobby to remember him.

Princes Street, Edinburgh.

The new part of Edinburgh has big streets with many shops. Visitors like to buy things to take home that have been made in Scotland.

Lots of visitors go to the zoo. Edinburgh Zoo has the biggest home for penguins in the world. In winter it can get very cold in Scotland, but penguins don't mind the snow!

Portobello Beach, Edinburgh.

Edinburgh is by the sea. Every day a gun in the castle goes off at one o'clock. Long ago the gun was to tell ships out at sea what the time was.

There is a beach near to the city. In summer, people can go to the fun fair on the beach.

The Tattoo at Edinburgh Castle.

Every summer there is a big festival in Edinburgh. People go to see plays and shows. Soldiers put on a big show at the castle. At the end of the festival there are fireworks. People come from all over the world to go to the Edinburgh festival.

The festival fireworks at Edinburgh Castle.